CHICAGO PUBLIC LIBRARY . Humboldt Park Branch
1605 N. Troy Street . Chicago . Illinois . 60647
Telephone . 312-744-2244
Library Hours
Monday-Thursday, 9 am- 8 pm
Friday & Saturday, 9 am-5 pm
Sunday, closed

Bajo las olas/Under the Sea

Cangrejos/Crabs

por/by Jody Sullivan Rake

Traducción/Translation: Dr. Martín Luis Guzmán Ferrer
Editor Consultor/Consulting Editor: Dra. Gail Saunders-Smith

Consultor/Consultant: Debbie Nuzzolo, Education Manager
SeaWorld, San Diego, California

Capstone press

Mankato, Minnesota

Pebble Plus is published by Capstone Press,
151 Good Counsel Drive, P.O. Box 669, Mankato, Minnesota 56002.
www.capstonepress.com

1 2 3 4 5 6 13 12 11 10 09 08

Library of Congress Cataloging-in-Publication Data
Rake, Jody Sullivan.
    [Crabs. Spanish & English]
    Cangrejos / por Jody Sullivan Rake = Crabs / by Jody Sullivan Rake.
    p. cm. — (Bajo las olas = Under the sea)
    Includes index.
    ISBN-13: 978-1-4296-2284-4 (hardcover)
    ISBN-10: 1-4296-2284-9 (hardcover)
    1. Crabs — Juvenile literature. I. Title. II. Title: Crabs. III. Series.
QL444.M33S9418 2009
595.3'86 — dc22   2008001450

Summary: Simple text and photographs present crabs, where they live, how they look, and what they do —
    in both English and Spanish.

Editorial Credits
Martha E. H. Rustad and Aaron Sautter, editors; Katy Kudela, bilingual editor; Eida del Risco, Spanish copy
    editor; Juliette Peters, set designer; Kate Opseth, book designer; Kelly Garvin, photo researcher;
    Scott Thoms, photo editor

Photo Credits
Bruce Coleman Inc./Masa Ushioda/V&W, 18–19
Corbis/Lawson Wood, cover
Marty Snyderman, 1, 5
Michael Patrick O'Neill, 17
Pete Carmichael, 14–15
Peter Arnold, Inc./Heinz Plenge, 9
Seapics.com/James D. Watt, 6–7; Ralf Kiefner, 21
Tom Stack & Associates, Inc./Dave Fleetham, 10–11; John Gerlach, 13

Note to Parents and Teachers

The Bajo las olas/Under the Sea set supports national science standards related to the
diversity and unity of life. This book describes and illustrates crabs in both English and
Spanish. The images support early readers in understanding the text. The repetition of
words and phrases helps early readers learn new words. This book also introduces early
readers to subject-specific vocabulary words, which are defined in the Glossary section.
Early readers may need assistance to read some words and to use the Table of Contents,
Glossary, Internet Sites, and Index sections of the book.

Table of Contents

Tabla de contenidos

What Are Crabs?

Crabs are sea animals
with hard shells.

¿Qué son
los cangrejos?

Los cangrejos son animales
marinos de caparazón duro.

Some crabs are larger than
a person. Other crabs are
as small as a ladybug.

Algunos cangrejos son más
grandes que una persona.
Otros cangrejos son tan
pequeños como una mariquita.

Body Parts

Crabs have eight legs.

They walk sideways.

Las partes del cuerpo

Los cangrejos tienen ocho patas. Los cangrejos caminan de lado.

Crabs have two sharp pincers.
Crabs catch small animals
with their pincers.

Los cangrejos tienen
dos tenazas muy filosas.
Los cangrejos atrapan
animales con sus tenazas.

pincers/
tenazas

Crabs have hard shells.
Their shells keep them
safe from other animals.

Los cangrejos tienen
un caparazón duro. Sus
caparazones los protegen
de otros animales.

Crabs have two eyes.
They can pull their
eyes into their shells.

Los cangrejos tienen dos
ojos. Los cangrejos pueden
meter los ojos dentro
de sus caparazones.

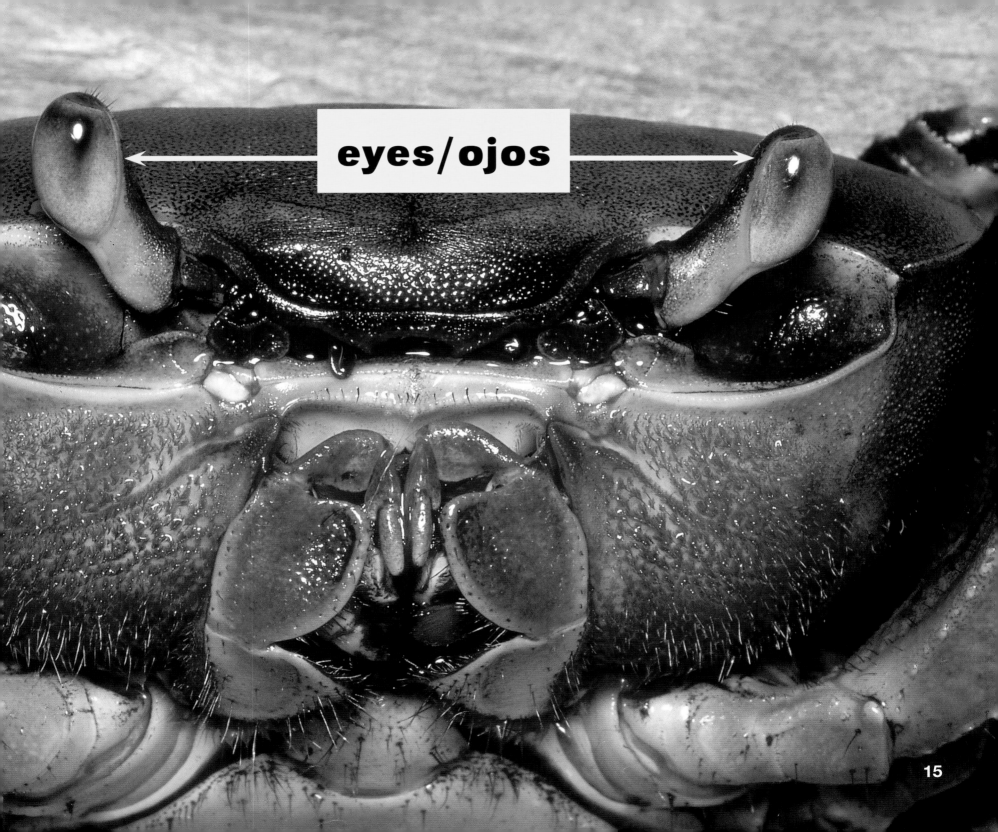

eyes/ojos

What Crabs Do

Some crabs hide from other animals. They cover themselves with small shells and seaweed.

Lo que hacen los cangrejos

Algunos cangrejos se esconden de otros animales. Se cubren con conchitas y con algas marinas.

Crabs use their pincers
to fight. Crabs fight
each other for mates.

Los cangrejos usan sus tenazas
para pelear. Los cangrejos
se pelean entre sí para
conseguir pareja.

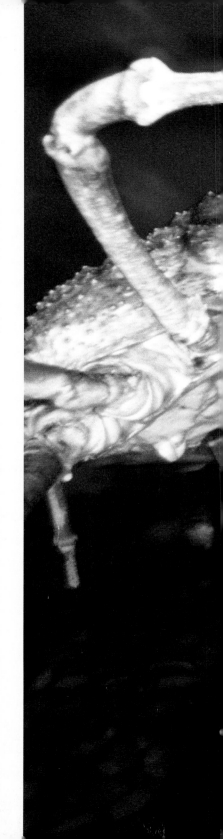

Under the Sea

Crabs live on the shore
and under the sea.

Bajo las olas

Los cangrejos viven en
la costa o bajo las olas.

Glossary

mate — a male or female partner of a pair of animals

pincer — a pinching claw; crabs use their pincers to eat and to fight.

seaweed — a plant that grows underwater

shell — a hard outer covering; a shell protects an animal from harm.

shore — the edge of the sea, where the water meets the land; shores are covered with sand and rocks; crabs sometimes live on the shore.

sideways — from side to side

Glosario

el alga marina — planta que crece bajo el agua

caminar de lado — moverse lateralmente, no de frente ni hacia atrás

el caparazón — cubierta dura que protege el cuerpo de ciertos animales

la costa — el borde del mar, donde el agua se junta con la tierra; las costas están cubiertas de arena o de rocas; los cangrejos algunas veces viven en la costa.

la pareja — compañero o compañera de un animal

la tenaza — pinza para sujetar; los cangrejos usan sus pinzas para comer y para pelear.

Internet Sites

FactHound offers a safe, fun way to find Internet sites related to this book. All of the sites on FactHound have been researched by our staff.

Here's how:

1. Visit *www.facthound.com*

2. Choose your grade level.

3. Type in this book ID **1429622849** for age-appropriate sites. You may also browse subjects by clicking on letters, or by clicking on pictures and words.

4. Click on the **Fetch It** button.

FactHound will fetch the best sites for you!

Index

Sitios de Internet

FactHound te brinda una manera divertida y segura de encontrar sitios de Internet relacionados con este libro. Hemos investigado todos los sitios de FactHound. Es posible que algunos sitios no estén en español.

Se hace así:

1. Visita *www.facthound.com*

2. Elige tu grado escolar.

3. Introduce este código especial **1429622849** para ver sitios apropiados a tu edad, o usa una palabra relacionada con este libro para hacer una búsqueda general.

4. Haz un clic en el botón **Fetch It**.

¡FactHound buscará los mejores sitios para ti!

Índice